ATTENTION AND ACTION

THE ADELSBERGER APPROACH TO MARKETING

KEVIN ADELSBERGER

ADELSBERGERMARKETING.COM

Published by Adelsberger Marketing

Jackson, Tennessee

Attention and Action - The Adelsberger
Approach to Marketing

Copyright © 2021

ISBN: 9780578842943
ISBN Ebook: 9780578842950

Cover Design: Ricky Santos

Layout: Kevin Adelsberger

Editors:

Renae Adelsberger
Brittany Crockett
Dan Phillips

To Renae without whom this business wouldnt exist and to the O.G. team members Ricky and Brittany who put in so much to help this business grow.

Contents

CHAPTER 1
OPENING THOUGHTS

Marketing is something everyone does throughout their lives. In childhood you may have been selling candy bars to raise money for school. That was marketing. Trying to pick up a date? That is a form of marketing. Working to grow a business? That requires marketing. Marketing is something we have been doing as a company since 2014. I (Kevin Adelsberger) love marketing. I love the challenge of it, the creativity of it, and the reward of helping someone solve the problems their organization faces.

There has never been a better or more complicated time to be in marketing. Even for us in the marketing industry, it's easy to get lost in all the options, sometimes even within one platform.

The simplest definition of marketing that I have is this:

Marketing is the effort of getting someone's attention and motivating them to take your call to action/goal.

This also applies to this book; it has three goals:

For new staff at Adelsberger Marketing, the goal of this book is to grab their attention and cause them to get a better grasp of the way we approach marketing. We want to prepare them to work on strategies and executions for our customers.

For potential customers, the goal of this book is to grab their attention with a free resource and either:

(1) get them to sign up for our email list which provides us an opportunity to market to them repeatedly and keep us on the top of their mind or

(2) look through this book and realize that marketing is a huge operation and know it is something they need help to do well. Additionally, if they realize they need help, they see this book and think, "if they know this much, they are the right people to go with! And even - "If they are sharing this, what aren't they sharing?"

And for SEO, one of the more recent strategies for search engine marketing is building content clusters that help express subject matter expertise to Google. The goal of these expert content clusters is to help us continue to rank well and potentially rank higher than our competitors so that we can win more business.

All three of these goals help further our business

and give us a great place to start talking about marketing. During the rest of the book we will talk about all aspects of marketing in our world today.

I wanted to open with general thoughts to set some mental framework for the rest of the book. One of the age-old questions we wrestle with is: Where does marketing start and sales take over?

Marketing vs Sales

The gap between marketing and sales is often a small crack in small organizations. However, that gap is more like a wide gulf in large organizations.

The size difference is a result of the broad definition of marketing. We believe, in short, marketing enables sales to happen. Marketing includes all the things that lead someone to be ready to make a purchase. Is a brochure sales? No. Can it enable sales? Yes.

Marketing helps generate sales. If someone comes across your brochure and then picks up a phone and calls you or visits your website to buy something - then mission accomplished! It helped create sales. Where this line gets fuzzy are things like eCommerce websites. Where does the line get drawn there? There are many elements of marketing on an eCommerce website: the photos, the copy, the branding, and the way the website works. But the actual transaction is sales.

Why does this matter? It's important to know who is responsible for what. If your sales teams need something to help enable sales, marketing should be responsive to that. If it's a new sales slide show or a new landing page on the website, those are tools that marketing can provide to help sales be successful.

Working with an outside marketing agency can be self-defeating if you are horrible at sales. Bad sales skills can kill good marketing. Likewise, bad marketing slows good sales. To help everyone be successful, we need to ensure open communication between marketing and sales. We need to help ensure each part is doing a good job with their tasks and that they are not afraid to ask for help.

In each organization, it is important to break down the goals of each department. In marketing, is the goal to generate leads for sales to then follow up with? Is it to grow the public perception of the organization? Is it to generate eCommerce sales? In your organization, it will be important to specify where sales and marketing mesh and who is responsible for what. The smaller the organization, the more cross over happens, especially when the CEO/Owner is responsible for all of it.

Attention

Attention is one of our more important resources we have left. But as a culture, we have not yet started treating it as essential as time. Attention can be garnered in a multitude of ways: bright colors, billboards, attractive people, cute dogs (and ugly dogs), notifications, emails, tv ads, and newspaper articles. While evaluating these multitudes of ways, one should also consider whose attention you are trying to gain and at what cost.

Gathering attention and reselling it is the principle that media companies are based on. Facebook isn't the product, we are. Facebook gathers our attention by showing us things we think are interesting and fostering a sense of community with people we may not see every day. We are the product because it sells our attention to advertisers. Newspapers gather attention by producing journalism and then sell that attention for advertising. I think for businesses that having an app will be standard in the future because the ability to have push notifications on the consumer's device/watch/glasses/other wearable technology will be a key attention-getter in a noisy world (call our friends at Sodium Halogen https://www.sodiumhalogen.com/ for custom app development).

The cost of gaining attention has never been higher which means that we as a culture are more distracted than ever. As a result, it can make it harder to get good attention from your audience (it's a painful cycle). We should think about the cost of each medium we are trying to use to get attention. Right now, the most affordable methods of getting attention are generally digital. There will come a day when the cost of digital ads will rise and the cost of traditional advertising will come down. Because of the current state of prices, we almost never recommend our clients purchase traditional advertising. There will be a day when the cost of traditional advertising has dropped enough to make it competitive with digital again. It is important to remember: Marketing is about attention, not necessarily about the platform of how we get that attention.

It is also important to consider whose attention you want. Understanding your customer is crucial to getting the right attention. If you primarily sell hemorrhoid cream to senior citizens, the attention that a tiktok influencer gathers is probably not the attention you want to pay for. Study: Who buys our product/service? What are they paying attention to?

What do they find valuable? How do we talk to them and get their attention? We will talk more about this later in this chapter.

An additional cost of garnering attention is the cost of trust or social capital. We can see this most clearly with "click bait" headlines online. If we do something extremely bold to gain attention and do not back it up with value, we will erode the trust that our audience has with us. The only exception to this rule seems to be state and national level party politics. You can see this in email marketing as well. If you subscribe to an email list and it proves to be annoying, you do not continue to open those emails. Also, as a society, companies continue to push the edges further and further to get and keep attention. There is an atrophying of the minimum level of excitement required to get and keep attention. This is a cost we and all of our children will pay for.

Builders and Drivers

When we consider working with a client and when someone considers their marketing resources using two categories, builders and drivers, is helpful. This is a concept we are borrowing from Paul Roetzer and PR 20/20. Builders are pieces of marketing that are "evergreen." "Evergreen" is a marketing term that means, like an evergreen tree, it doesn't go out of season. It also has a long shelf life and, much like your house, it is a fairly permanent fixture. Drivers are more temporary and like sunflowers, they are only good for a season. (Sunflowers are an annual plant, I am told.)

Builders are great places to start when thinking about marketing. Builders require some investment but allow your team to be successful for a long time. A Website is a builder; it's evergreen. A hero video is a builder, if done properly. We want to have builders because it helps establish yours as a business worth working with. Builders will provide value for a long time - they are an investment. Examples of builders:

- Website
- Hero Video
- Email Marketing System
- Value Providing Ebook
- Sales Deck
- Branding Elements
- Business Cards
- Brochure

Drivers are what help motivate people to go to your builders. Examples of drivers:

- Social Media Content
- Digital Ads
- TV Ads
- Blog Post
- PR Piece

Investing in drivers without having good builders in place is where lots of customers want to start, but it's a short-sighted strategy. If you drive someone to a low-quality builder, you are likely going to put a customer off. Invest in builders first, then create drivers to continue to help build a business.

Providing Value

Many of the best versions of marketing provide value. Value in this instance has a really broad definition. Value could be: something that is funny, something that makes you feel good, or something that educates. We like to suggest to many of our customers that providing education is always a good idea. When you provide education to your customers, in business to business (B2B) or business to consumer (B2C), you will gain a few things:

Evergreen Content- If you educate your customers, that content is evergreen. A restaurant talking about a weekend special is only valuable to the audience for a limited amount of time. A restaurant doing an explainer about what certain terms mean on their menu or how to select the best steaks provides value and is relevant for a long period of time. These pieces can also be reused over time without much reinvention.

Higher Value- If you are able to educate your customers on why things are valuable to them, you increase your own value. If an accounting business is able to talk about how certain business structures can end up saving owners money, they are at the same time increasing the value of their services in the customer's mind. Sometimes people do not understand that full value proposition of a good or service. If you can educate someone about the full value, you might take them to a place where they are willing to pay more for that good or service than they would have previously paid. Saddleback Leather does a great job about educating customers on their quality which helps them charge high amounts for their products.

Positioning as an Expert- This might be the most valuable component of education. The more you are able to demonstrate your expertise to your audience, the more you will be viewed as an expert in the industry. People like hiring experts. Being the top in your field means extra money for you. Being seen as an expert on a subject in your geographical area leads to free marketing opportunities and the increase of reputation leads to more business.

SEO Value- Educational content usually answers questions for customers. Answering questions is a key component of Search Engine Optimization (SEO) marketing. When you create content that has informational aspects to it, you will likely end up adding keywords to those posts that will help your potential customers find you on Search Engines.

Permission-Based Marketing and Interruption Based Marketing

As so brilliantly pointed out by Seth Godin in his book, *Permission Marketing*, we need to understand the difference between permission and interruption based marketing.

Traditionally all marketing was interruption

based. It is called an "interruption" because it breaks up the content you were intentionally looking for. You are watching tv and *boom* interruption with an ad. Driving down the road enjoying a scenic view and *boom* billboard (unless you are in South Dakota. THERE ARE BILLBOARDS EVERYWHERE IN SOUTH DAKOTA). The advertising is interrupting the experience you are having. Entire industries are based on interruption advertising. All tv, radio, and most newspapers and magazines are based on interruption advertising.

Of course, the internet is largely focused on this as well. Most digital advertising is interruption based. News websites use display advertising to generate revenue. YouTube plays preroll and midroll ads to keep your attention for its advertisers.

Certain sections in the online economy are suffering because there are also forces trying to prevent digital ads from showing on your computer. The Ad Blocking industry is huge and growing with people being willing to pay for ads to be removed from their web experience. One estimate says that up to 25.8 percent of internet users were using ad blockers in 2019 (https://www.statista.com/statistics/804008/ad-blocking-reach-usage-us/). Industries that are designed for interruption marketing are already struggling to survive in our modern world. For users to prevent a few ads hurts the news and content sources we enjoy to consume. Imagine running an ad supported business and having 25% of our audience get the content and not "pay" by blocking ads. We will increasingly see subscription only content models for things we are used to looking at for free. There will be a technological arms race to figure out how to make this viable. Before the dust is settled and some sort of equilibrium is reached, there will be many sources of great content lost to the history pages in wikipedia.

Permission marketing however is the opposite of interruption marketing. Permission marketing is called permission because the customer has given us permission to talk to them. This spans lots of media: print newsletters, emails, text messages, and some forms of social media. But the key here is that with permission, we contact these customers. We can help create loyal customers for life if we work with permission marketing.

Permission marketing works with existing customers. Interruption marketing works to help bring in new customers. It takes both kinds. But if we can, we push clients to work on permission marketing first. If you are able to maximize the value of existing customers, you are setting yourself up for huge success in business.

Awareness and Direct Response Marketing

Two final categories we need to consider when we think about marketing is awareness and direct response marketing. While these two ideas can work together in many contexts, I usually see them in contrast with each other. A simple way to define these are: awareness as "aren't we cool and will make your life better" and direct response as "buy this thing here, now preferably." There is certainly some crossover between the ideas as we will look at below, but the two approaches are very different. We use these levels of awareness not as a hard and fast rule but helpful categories in what we are trying to communicate.

When we think about our customers, we need to realize there are levels of awareness each of them has. Awareness breaks down like this (inspired by *Breakthrough Advertising* by Eugene Schwartz)

1. Customers who don't know your product or don't know that they need your product. (Awareness)

2. Customers who don't know your product but know that a need for your type of product

exists. (Awareness)

3. Customers who are aware of your product and know that they have a need for your project. (Awareness/Direct Response)

4. Customers who are ready to buy your product but have not yet. (Direct Response)

When we have a customer who hits level 3 and 4, we need to use direct response advertising to help drive sales. Direct response is like the coupons you get in the mail from restaurants or walking through a mall and seeing a "50% off" sign in the window. It even includes offering the product on sale for a limited amount of time. These ads create a response directly from the customer. These ads are very trackable, especially online with UTM parameters (UTM Parameters are the way Google Analytics can read web addresses to show where website traffic came from. UTM stands for Urchin Tracking Module which is the company that Google bought to acquire this technology). With UTM parameters, you can see a customer's journey very clearly.

When you are talking to customers in level 1 and sometimes level 2 of awareness, you need to be focused on awareness marketing. Awareness marketing is sometimes grouped together with brand marketing. The goal of awareness marketing is to ensure that as people learn about your product/ service, they understand what it's for, who it's for, and what it stands for. That will help them go from steps 1 or 2 to step 4.

When working with marketing to groups of people, taking the opportunity to work on both ends of the spectrum will allow your business to win over the long run and help build a funnel of customers. However, certain companies will only play in either end of that pool. The closer your product gets to commodity status, the closer it will get to always needing to do direct response in mass marketing efforts. The more premium the branding, the more likely they are to stay in the awareness branding. For example, Apple almost always runs awareness campaigns through tv and online media. Oil changes and fast food are almost always direct response marketing through mailers and tv.

You will not likely see a generic mailer with coupons from Apple in your mailbox. You will likely see them online or on tv with an ad that paints a picture of a cool or better life with their product. While you will see some restaurants paint a cool life picture, it almost always ends with "$6.99 at participating restaurants."

These are some broad thoughts on marketing. Before you start marketing, you should figure out what you are marketing, more on that in chapter 2.

In Chapter 1, we talked about "what is marketing?" In this chapter, we will turn the focus to where the process should begin - with you. If you do business with a good marketing agency, almost all of them will start with some sort of discovery process. Some may call it a brainstorm or Strategy Workshop (like our friends at Sodium Halogen). Regardless of name, the agency uses this activity to learn about your business so they know how to best communicate with your market. If they're really good, they'll focus on value for the customer, not just what you want to talk about.

In our experience, the best clients are usually the ones who have spent time thinking about the "know thyself" components before they come to the table with us. If they haven't, we think it through with them. Knowing thyself allows you to communicate clearly. Whether that communication is internally to staff and stakeholders or externally to potential and current customers, without a clear picture of yourself, it is difficult to communicate effectively.

Who are you? Mission/Vision/ Purpose

One of my favorite jokes from the TV show

Scrubs involves a character described as "Johnny the tackling Alzheimer's patient." (https://www.youtube.com/watch?v=3kx7tgkJbjo) Johnny yells, "Who am I?!?" as he tackles the protagonist, JD. Many businesses act the same way. They have done enough to start making sales, or tackling, but they are not sure who they are, which makes it difficult to grow beyond their base. When you do not understand who you are, you will waste time chasing ideas that do not fit with you rather than investing in the things that will make your company great.

When you consider who you are as a business, you need to get beyond the desire to make money and get into why you do what you do. Some businesses only want to make money, but they need to develop a self identity beyond that goal to build relationships with customers.

At Adelsberger Marketing, we like to request the mission or vision statements from our clients. The clients who have one show they are thinking about both the big picture and how to become the best organization that they can.

A good mission statement states what the end goal of the organization is. A good mission statement contains four key elements:

    1. Concise- A good mission statement is not

a paragraph long. It's one - maybe two - sentences. The more concise you can make it, the more effective it will be. Concentrate on your core purpose, not a strategy or a set of tactics. Strategy is a level of planning that affects things like where you place your ads. Tactics are more granular such as using certain dimensions on video exports to maximize value for each social channel. In World War II, the Allies' mission was to defeat the Axis powers. The strategy was to invade Europe from North and South and the tactics involved things like storming the beaches of Normandy. Mission statements must stay above the frame of strategy and tactics.

2. Memorable- Memorability is important because it allows the mission to sink into the language of the team and affect their judgement. A good, memorable mission statement, consistently preached by leadership can help infect a team with that mission.

3. Timeless- Occasionally you will come across a mission statement that mentions specific methods for completing your mission. This is a common error. Look at the World War II example again: strategies and tactics change over time. (The obvious exception of this would be a mission statement that was for an organization that was time sensitive or limited in scope

like an election campaign.) Methods, strategies, and tactics change. If your organization survives for any period of time, you do not want to rebuild your mission statement every few years.

4. Focusing- Organizations are presented with a variety of opportunities. It can be difficult to sort these choices out. A solid mission statement can help an organization evaluate and find all the good ideas that come to it. When considering new opportunities or plans, look back to the mission statement and ask: "Does this opportunity fit with the mission statement? Does it prevent us from doing the things that are already helping us accomplish this mission?"

These are a few mission statements that I have helped write. I feel like they satisfy the above qualities:

Our Jackson Home: To tell the stories of the people and the city that we all love.

STAR Center: To help any person, with any disability, to realize their potential.

Adelsberger Marketing: To make creative work that grows our clients' businesses, in a culture that values our team and community.

Vision statements are slightly different. Vision statements look ahead to what the world would look like if the organization is able to complete its mission. These are generally less important to an organization than a mission statement. It doesn't hurt to have both, but if you only have time for one, go with the mission statement. I recently helped write this vision statement for Madison County CASA (Court Appointed Special Advocates):

We provide a volunteer voice for all abused and neglected children in the West Tennessee Juvenile Court System.

Price/Position/Product/Place

Now that we have covered who you are, we can start to get a better understanding of where you sit in the marketplace. The classic reason for doing this is building out what is often referred to as the "Four P's." They are: product, price, place, and promotion. They are important to evaluate as you start investing in marketing. There are entire books written on this topic alone, but we are going to take a quick look at each of these:

Product- What is it that you are selling? Is it good? How good is it? What makes it special?

Price- How much is your product? Is it expensive for the market? Is it cheap for the market? Do you use coupons or would that hurt your brand? (Also, you are probably not charging enough.)

Place- How are customers getting access to this product? I imagine this answer was much simpler when the concept of the Four P's was created.

Promotion- How are you going to communicate it? Are competitors communicating in certain ways? Are there any no-no's for your industry? What have you already tried and was it successful?

Do you deliver well?

If you spend $10,000 on advertising and your customer service or product is horrible, what will the result be? You'll have wasted that $10k and then some. Why? First impressions matter more to a person than just about anything else. If you fail to deliver on your products and your customer service is horrible, people will tell other people. In the social media age, that is even more true. Even the best brands have naysayers online because it costs so little to leave a bad review. It costs almost nothing socially and it is free to run your name through the mud or sing your praises online. You also lose out on the potential of repeat business which is the lifeblood of most businesses.

You need to ensure your product is ready for the stage before you put a spotlight on it. Customer service is an investment worth making. Have you stress tested your product, your delivery method, and your customer service? What would happen to your business if 10 more customers than usual called tomorrow? What about 50 more? What if 3 more had a bad experience? Considering these things and planning for them is crucial to success in marketing.

One of my favorite books on customer service is: *Customers for Life* by Carl Sewell. I was on a trip to Texas with my wife when our Subaru started acting funny. We stopped in the local Subaru dealer on a Friday afternoon and desperately asked for help so that we could return home that night. This local dealer was a Sewell dealer and they went above and beyond from every level, so I left them a good review online. While looking them up, I found the owner's book and it did not disappoint.

Investing in customer service is investing in your customers. It will help grow repeat business which is more affordable than investing in new customers.

Stark Raving Fans

"Stark Raving Fans" is a term that I came across in Seth Godin's work. Stark Raving Fans means you go beyond just customer service to seeing every interaction with a customer as a chance to turn them into a marketing channel. If you are so good that your customers love doing business with you, they will tell others. If you make Stark Raving Fans of your business, they will help you grow. How do you create them? By doing business the right way. Under promise and over deliver. Deliver on time. And if something does go wrong, make it right (even if it costs you financially). When we stop seeing customers as a transaction and start seeing them as people and investments in our future, we create Stark Raving Fans.

Messaging and Terminology

The way we talk about things can be important to

convey what they mean to us. Calling someone who works in your organization a team member rather than an employee may seem trivial, but it can send a different message. When we work with a company, it is important for us to understand why they use certain terminology. Additionally, they might never have outlined for the organization which words to use and why. In some cases, it can make a huge difference. When beginning the marketing process, it's important to talk through what words we use for which things. Defining the words and terms that are important to your brand can even be part of your branding process with an agency. If you want your "team" to use the word "customers" instead of "patients" then you have to weave those terms into the fabric of your business. Another example would be a personnel company who refers to its staffers as "associates" instead of "temps." It has a different ring to it and can help direct the parts of your company to treat those people differently.

It is also important to share those terms and meanings with your marketing partners. Using those words internally is one thing, but making sure that the use of those words is consistent externally is also important. The words you use paint a picture of your company to the world.

Who are your customers?

You need to know who your customers are in order to grow a business. We start every project with an exercise to help us create "avatars" (also known as Personas or Customer Profiles) that represent our customers. Picking out a few of the major types of customers for your business and thinking through their wants and needs allows you to better engage these customers. But also you need to understand their levels of awareness. *Breakthrough Advertising* by Eugene Schwartz does a great job of breaking this down; but the book costs several hundred dollars. So here is a bit of a summary. First, we break customers down into four groups:

- Customers who don't know your product or that they need your product

- Customers who don't know your product but know that a need for your product exists

- Customers who are aware of your product and they have a need

- Customers who are ready to buy your product but have not yet

You need to treat each of these customer awareness groups separately. An ad for converting group 4 while they are in your store will work less effectively on someone in group 1. You can read more about this in Chapter 1. Map these stages out and let them influence when and where you communicate.

CHAPTER 3
BRANDING AND BUILDERS

When we work on marketing projects, we like to think of two categories: Builders and Drivers. Builders are things that we make that have a long lifespan. These are our fundamentals, the blocking and tackling of marketing. Nailing these components sets you up for success, looks professional, prepares you to convert inbound leads, and pays dividends in the long run. When you see an Apple or Nike Ad, you know they are an Apple or Nike advertisement. Their style is part of their brand. Companies that work on design are more successful than those who don't, according to McKinsey (https://www.mckinsey.com/business-functions/mckinsey-design/our-insights/the-business-value-of-design#). When establishing a brand, followingare elements that every company should have and have in good order.

Branding (Logo, Fonts, Colors)

Branding is a fundamental part of any business and every company should have a good logo as part of the brand. Branding is a term that has a lot of different meanings depending on who you talk to; so we are going to define it. A brand is all the ways your company is represented to the world. Branding is the use of your logo and the imagery/materials that go with it. There are three key parts to branding: Logo, Fonts, and Colors.

Logo- The masthead of your company, the sign that, when used properly, people in your community will know over time and instantly connect with your company. A good logo can help raise the value of your company and raise the expectations of your service, which can allow you to charge more. A good logo should be memorable, work in one color, and work in all sizes. Will it look good both on letterhead and also on a billboard? Now we even need to think about how the logo will look when it's tiny on your phone. Think about the Favicon, the icon a website puts in your web browser's tab to represent your website- will your branding work there? Think about where you will need to use the logo. Different mediums and uses may affect the design of the logo. A good logo will also not require updating every few years, so it's worth investing in to get a good one made.

Fonts- To achieve consistency in use across design applications, certain fonts should be used repeatedly. For our company, the Gotham font makes a lot of appearances. Within fonts, there are sometimes different weights that make differentiating information much easier. Oftentimes, when a legitimate design company delivers a logo project, they will also deliver a family of logos and a guide on how to use them. Refer to these. If you do not have one, develop a guide of fonts to use. These do not have to be the same fonts as in the logo, but sometimes they will be.

Colors- Like fonts, colors are something that should be used consistently across the branding of a company. If your primary colors are red and blue, hot pink will have a hard time working its way into marketing. But if your company's only color is Pink, like Lemonade Insurance or T-Mobile, you are going to see it in almost every element of their branding. Colors are more noticeable to the average consumer than fonts. It is important to be consistent over time. A good design company will provide you a family of colors to use when creating a logo.

Brand Identity Guide- All of these elements should be delivered to you in a branding identity guide and kit. We make sure our clients have all the logo files they need to use the logo without us, whether we were to get hit by a bus or they decided they didn't like us anymore. The brand guide should contain information on: Logo types, color schemes, font names, colors, color values, and potentially things like messaging and terminology.

Vector vs Raster- If you are reading this and are not a designer, you need to know the difference between a Vector and a Raster file. We run into this all the time: We ask clients for a logo file and they send us a .jpeg. There are few things that make a designer want to pull the hair out of their head faster. A .jpeg is a raster file. A raster file is a static image file that does not scale. It's almost like it's printed on paper. If you stretch the paper, it will rip. In digital terms, it will pixelate and look horrible. A vector file is an image file that uses math to keep all the elements in proper proportion to each other. If you stretch it, it will expand and look great. A vector graphic usually comes with the following file formats: .svg, .eps, .ai and sometimes they are saved in .pdf. Rasters have their place. But do all designers a favor and learn where your vectors are saved and send those to people. We suggest you save them in a Google Drive or Dropbox folder that has your logo kit in it so that you can quickly send a link to any vendor.

Messaging Elevator Pitch

The classic imaginative scenario, you wind up on an elevator with a potential customer or investor and you get 60 seconds (or less) and what do you say? Do you bumble through it or do you crush it? I hope you crush it. However, unless you are exceptionally good on your feet, without a prepared elevator pitch, you might be in trouble. So how do we come up with an elevator pitch? I think one of the greatest resources for this is StoryBrand by Donald Miller. The main concept of StoryBrand is that when you are thinking about messaging for your business, you need to think about how to make your customer the hero of the story and your business the guide that will help that hero succeed. A short marketing message should address, at the minimum: who you help and how you help them.

For Adelsberger Marketing, we realized that most of our customers come to us because they are having problems with digital marketing. They are either confused about what to do, scared to do something about it, or realize they do not have enough time to do it right. We wanted to position ourselves as the expert they come to help guide them through digital marketing. Ultimately we want them to succeed at digital marketing with our help. Our logo is a shield which invokes some fierceness, so we say, "We lead businesses to conquer digital marketing." We then follow up with some ways we do that for people. I frequently add on to that core message based on who I am speaking to. If it's a company I feel like needs our design services, then I start talking about who we have helped recently in that service area.

When thinking about a marketing message, we need to consider what our customer needs from us, not necessarily what we want to brag about. I may want to brag about our newest camera gear, but most customers don't care. They only care how I solve their problems. Your marketing messaging should reflect that.

Our recommendation would be that you have a one to two line marketing message and a somewhat longer paragraph that both you and your team can spit out at any moment. When working on a longer form pitch, get into more details like: specific services lists, success stories, and notable client lists.

Once you have your basic messaging, it is important to keep it consistent across all your builders and drivers. You may highlight different aspects for different elements of your drivers, but for the most part, you will come back to this well of messaging again and again.

Graphic Elements (Collateral)

When making sure you have all the builders in place, it is not necessarily exciting to think about all the many graphic elements that one might need to have on hand. Here is a list of essentials:

-Business Card

-Letterhead

-Signage

-Slideshow Template

-Notecard (you should be writing notes to people)

-Brochure/Sales Card

-Email Signature

-Facebook Profile Image

-Facebook Cover Image

-Twitter Profile Image

-Twitter Cover Image

-YouTube Profile Image

-YouTube Cover Image

-Other social media profiles

-Social Media Template Image

-Video Logo Reveal

-Video Branding (Lower third, information

screen, transitions)

-Email Marketing Template

Having consistent branding through all of these elements will allow you to have clarity in message and professionalism throughout your marketing. This will help you leave no doubt that customers are dealing with a professional organization. Also, an important note for all the social media channels: test these on mobile. Often these social channels change the crop of the image when on mobile so test it on both before committing to it. Additionally, social media profile icons are tiny on mobile devices so be sure to minimize what is in the image.

Imagery/Photography

The world's largest companies have detailed photography standards for marketing. They will have entire guides dedicated to how their products should look, who should be included in photos, and even what types of situations the photos should show. While you might not have a giant library of photography rules, you should consider some broad thoughts about selecting imagery for your company:

Diversity- One of the biggest faux paus we see when working companies is failure to include diversity in their messaging visually. When working with a company or a community that has a diverse customer base/collection of service providers, it's important to reflect that in the marketing materials. This will sometimes require intentionality on the part of the customer and the photo provider.

Connections- What do you want to be associated with?- When doing styled shoots or selecting community sourced images, we need to evaluate what we want to be associated with. If you do a photoshoot with someone wearing a six shooter on their hip, you should ask yourself, does your brand want to be connected to guns? I use that example because the reaction normally goes strongly one way or another. If you are using community generated content, you may want to do a quick look on the social profiles of those submitting content. This may help you flag potential trouble spots before they arise.

Quality of the photos- Do you want highly polished stock photos or are you looking for images that feel a little more organic. This will guide your selection of stock photos or investment in local photography.

Sizes- If you do not tell photographers what size of photos you want, they will deliver you whatever size they want to. It's a good idea to plan ahead. Think about what you want in return for working with a photographer.

Color Themes- If you go for a highly styled version of photography for your company, you may want to have a lot of a specific color involved in the shoot. Think of a company like T-Mobile; they have pink everywhere.

Outside Brands- When working with models or in a location, be sure to scan the photographs and sets for outside brands. People may be wearing a Nike shirt or have Nike shoes on. A party shoot might have specific brands of beer in the shoot. This may not be a problem for you, but it's something to consider. You never know when the next big brand will become toxic to your customer base.

Formal vs. Informal- When thinking about the setting of the photos, the wardrobe, the expressions on the faces of the people, ask: Are we going for formal or informal in our photos? Some companies may want a more formal looking photograph, while others opt for informal and fun. A lot has to do with who your customers are and how you position yourself in the market.

Website

In our society today, a website is a required part of any company's marketing success. There was a time when a website was optional and even today some point to social media profiles as being sufficient. But I think relying on a social media profile in lieu of a website, even a very small one, is short sighted.

Social media profiles and networks will come and go. They exist in a "walled kingdom." To fully experience a social media profile, you normally need to be active on the network. You will have customers who are not active on that network. When you create your business with a Facebook page only, you limit your reach to that network of social media users. You are also building on "rented land." Facebook and other social media platforms are going to push you to spend money for advertising by reducing your marketing effectiveness. Lastly, it also hurts your ability to show up on search engines. Search engines prefer real websites because they help them to index information and present the most helpful sites to their users. The top things we look for in a good website:

Important Information: Many people visit websites solely for the critical information like: address, phone number, business hours, and other contact information. This information should be READILY AVAILABLE, especially if you are a local business.

Additionally, we think there are a few more categories of essential information:

What do you do? What service do you offer and why should the customer buy it from you.

What does the process look like? How does working with you work? It helps answer a lot of questions the customer might have.

What do others say about you? Including reviews on your website can help provide social proof that doing business with you is a good idea. More detailed testimonials might also be helpful. And consider including headshots, photos, and project summaries and outcomes.

Be sure you include your accreditations and connections to important associations to show your legitimacy.

CTA- What is your call to action? When building a site, it's good to consider what you want a visitor to do. For our site, we have two: download our digital marketing checklist and schedule a meeting. We are not selling anything directly on our site, but we would love to build a relationship with a potential customer.

Mobile Friendly- This has been the standard for years now but it still needs to be said because we still get asked in the proposal process, "Will this work on my cell phone?" Web traffic is always increasing from mobile devices so if your site does not work well on a mobile device, you are missing out on lots of traffic.

SEO- SEO or Search Engine Optimization has evolved a lot over the years. Originally, SEO was done through blunt options like keyword stuffing. For example, if I put the word "marketing" on my homepage 1,000 times then I would be the top result in Google. But today, there are some clear things you should do to have good SEO, in no particular order:

Meta Tags- This is an SEO Classic. Make sure your meta tags are set up on at least your major pages. A meta tag is a short description that Search Engines use to get a quick description of the purpose of that page or site. It's best if all your pages have well written meta tags.

Mobile Friendly- Though this should be standard now, Google will lower your rating if your site does not work well on mobile devices. If your buttons are too big or your text gets cut off, Google can detect that and will penalize you for it.

Header Tags- H1, H2, and so on mean Header 1, Header 2. It is a way to break out information for those who are not seeing the styling on the website. For multiple reasons, including accessibility (the ability to access the website by those who need to use screen readers), it is important to have your text divided by H1 and H2 and more definers. It helps a screen reader (technology that reads websites to individuals with visual impairment) or a crawling bot (programs used by Search Engines to learn what your website is about) realize what is most important on your page.

Customer Focused- A site designed for humans with SEO in mind. You can certainly make a site that is only designed for SEO. In fact this used to be the standard for SEO. But this is no longer the case. Google has really focused on website structure and content that work for humans. They take signals of how people interact with your site to see if it's worthwhile or not. Keep SEO in mind as you design but as a secondary function.

Site Health- When you think about site health, one thing to think about is: how many of my internal links are working correctly or have other errors. If your site has broken internal links due to articles missing or domains being changed, that hurts the health. Is my SSL Certificate active and working on all pages, how is the site's load speed? Is my written content helpful? If your website is useful to humans, it will help on SEO. You might have been able to rank #1 for shoes in the past by cheating SEO but still you only sell socks. If people are looking for shoes and come to your site for socks, they will have a bad experience and it will hurt your results in the long run.

SSL- A Secure Socket Layer certificate is a security device that helps protect website traffic from prying eyes. Having an SSL is important now. It is almost like a badge of, "we know what we are doing" for Google. It also offers security value for your website which is why it started in e-commerce, but thanks to Google's influence, it has become a global standard.

Backlinks- Backlinks are one of the most valuable things you can invest in for your business's SEO rankings. Backlinks are links from other sources that help establish your site as authoritative, safe, or legitimate. Some easy examples of acquirable backlinks: Chambers of Commerce, Social Media Sites, blog submissions to other sites. Adding these backlinks over time will help your ranking on search engines and help increase your domain authority which is how valuable your site looks to search engines.

Google Tools- Google, while difficult to navigate some of its SEO algorithms, also provides free tools to help with the search results.

Google My Business: If you can do one thing after launching your site to help with SEO, it would be to fill out your Google My Business profile. This helps Google surface you and you even get to customize it.

Search Console- This is another fantastic, free tool by Google. You can submit sitemaps to help speed up the crawling by Google's bots. You can also get notifications about site problems for SEO. This is a great free application.

Site Speed- Becoming more important to Google is site speed. Google knows that experience is important to how useful a site so loading quickly affects your ranking. Google actually has its own PageSpeed Insights tool that you can find via a Google Search.

NAP Info is Correct- NAP information is Name, Address, Phone number. You want to make sure that the NAP information is consistent across your site and consistent with your Google My Business listing. If you are labeled as 742 Evergreen Terrace on your site and 742 Evergreen Tr. on Google My Business, you have a problem, make sure they are the same.

SEO Tools - We love AHREFS (ahrefs.com) as a tool that helps us manage many SEO research options. It does cost some money, but if you are serious about SEO improvement, you will need to invest in AHREFS or one of its competitors.

Content

Who is the content on your site for? It is for your customer. I repeat: It is for your customer. You need to think about what your customer wants and needs as you prepare content for your website. Frequently people will want to focus on things that they care about, not things that their customers care about. Why should they care about you? What do you provide for them? It's the benefit not the technical details. A pest control company provides a pest free environment, not necessarily ACME Formula 1027 Pest Control Spray. You might be very proud that you use ACME but unless that means something to the customer, it's not worth covering. However, if ACME is all natural and environmentally friendly, and won't hurt your kids or dog if they accidentally consume it, that is a benefit that would be worth mentioning.

Content also needs to be laid out in a way that

is easy to use. If you have some information that is accessed all the time, like location or phone number, make that easy to find and "above the fold." Above the fold means that it is visible when someone loads the website without scrolling. This term originated with newspapers because important stories were always printed above the bisectional fold of the newspaper, being the area that is shown first to the customer.

We encourage you to think about the personas (or avatars or customer profiles) of your customers and to think about what is important to those customers.

Imagery

Avoid stock photos if you can. People can spot them from a mile away. Real photos taken of a company create more authenticity which is a valuable commodity in our era. Keep your customer personas in mind as you develop imagery for the site. If your customer base is largely teenagers, you probably do not want to exclusively feature senior citizens on your site imagery. Site imagery should reflect your customer base and what their aspirations are.

Analytics

If you are running a website without Google Analytics on it, you are doing it wrong. Google Analytics is a free tool from Google that does a fantastic job of measuring website traffic. But beyond website traffic, it can also help show where traffic is coming from, what pieces of the website visitors are interacting with, and potentially where conversion traffic is coming from. This information can prove pivotal when deciding where to invest future dollars for the growth of your company.

Hero Video

Video has become a staple of any business that has an online presence. A hero video is the one video you want people to watch about your brand or product. We call it a hero video because it might be the best representation of you to the consumer. A hero video will cover the uniqueness of your company, your value proposition, possibly a bit of history, and will look good doing all these things. Ideally these videos will be 2-3 minutes in length so that they are not an enormous investment of time for someone learning who you are. Host this on Vimeo to prevent customers getting dragged elsewhere by suggested videos.

Lead Generation Tool

A freebie to help educate your audience is a great way to build some trust with your audience. For example, we put together a resource called "Digital Marketing Checklist." That document walks someone through the major areas of digital marketing and gives them a few points to start with to make sure they get off on the right foot. We believe it provides some value, without providing so much value that would make us not worth hiring. But it does start to establish a relationship with our potential customers. We usually require someone to submit an email address to receive our freebies. This leads to more emails for your email list, which can help you stay in touch with consumers on a regular basis for almost no cost.

Social Media Accounts

Establishing the social media accounts that will work best with your business and customers is worth time to do right. Start by examining your customer personas and see where they spend their time online. Also see where you and your team can invest time. Youtube might take a bit more time then you have available while instagram can be done fairly quickly. It's better to not have a channel then have one and abandon it. So consider the investment in time before you launch a new channel.

Google My Business Account

This can be overlooked by a business new to the online world, but a Google My Business account is absolutely key to being found locally online. Google My Business is a free tool created by Google to give you control over what information shows up when someone searches for you online. Google shows what the Google My Business listing has on it, so it's a key place to make sure things like hours and services are correct. This listing will have information whether you keep it updated or not, so it's best to take the time to claim it and update it. Protip: keep a running spreadsheet that has all the places with your NAP information so that, if it was ever to change, you would be able to change all the places in an efficient manner.

One thing we encourage almost all of our customers to do is pursue content marketing and positioning as an expert. What is content marketing? Content Marketing is the practice of creating helpful material that educates or entertains potential and existing customers to help build a deeper relationship with them. Positioning yourself or your company as an expert is along the same lines, but in this instance, the whole goal is to show your knowledge to the audience. These two plays allow you over time to build a good base for inbound lead generation.

Content Generation

The most difficult part of content marketing we have found is dedicating the time and brainspace to actually creating the content. Some of this can be manufactured by others. But for the content to be great it needs to originate with Subject Matter Experts. When working with busy clients, we will normally ask them to give us an outline of what they want to cover and we can usually take it from there or conduct an interview to get the information on paper. It's important to remember that most of this content is going to be evergreen, meaning that it will be valuable for a long time as opposed to seasonal advice.

One of the most common problems in communicating is the Burden of Knowledge. The Burden of Knowledge is a communication hazard that shows up when someone who is an expert in an area fails to realize that not everyone has the same knowledge. As a videographer, I may know that white balance and working in rooms with LED lights can be an issue, but I can forget that not everyone thinks that way. Those could be two tips to set forth in content to help people but I may miss it due to my burden of knowledge. This also works out in some of the terminology that we use. People who are not thinking about their Burden of Knowledge may tend to use industry jargon which could leave a casual observer or someone who is just learning about this field in the dark. When we work on our content, we want to make sure we remove traces of the Burden of Knowledge that our potential customers would be lacking.

One other key idea in content marketing is that hard sales are a "no go." You should use this information in a general way to show a better way to do things and lean on that knowledge. Trust that your material will naturally lead the audience to call you. Hard sales can jade an audience and undermine the content you are making.

Where do we get ideas for content marketing?

When working through ideas for content marketing, here are a few places to start: What are the ten most common questions that your sales people get asked? If the same questions come up repeatedly, this is an opportunity to make content around that subject. A second idea is to look at your customer personas and brainstorm what they care about. If you are an ice supplier and a specific customer persona cares about clear ice for display, you can generate content about how to make that kind of ice or the common issues in ice production. A brainstorming session to generate ideas for content is a great opportunity to get the whole team involved. Consider: What are things that make you or your business unique? What are things you do better or only have compared to others? What do your customers care about? What are things you would want to talk about at parties?

We would suggest a brainstorming activity (like a Mad Lib) that combines the emotion, the type of content, and the mediums directed at each of your customer personas to help develop content they would find valuable.

Maximize Content Usefulness

You can transform one blog post into a lot of pieces of content for social. From that one blog post, you could write a script for a video, pull out quotes to turn into graphic, use the blog as a start for a podcast, or even create an infographic. The great part about reusing this content is that you can bring others into it easily. If you as the subject matter expert create a thorough piece of content, turning it into a bunch of side pieces of content by a marketing team will be much easier than having them try to create the primary piece of content. We love to extract as much content as possible to maximize the value of the time invested into that content and to help reach as many people as possible. Gary Vaynerchuck, better known as Gary Vee, is the Owner of VaynerMedia and Founder of WineLibrary TV. He is one of the all time great Entrepreneurs of our era. His personal brand team are the sterling examples of this practice. Check him out online by looking for @GaryVee.

Speaking Engagements

If you get invited to a speaking engagement, you have been handed a tremendous opportunity. This might be harder if you are not skilled in public speaking but hopefully you will have a window in which to practice ahead of time. Speaking Engagements are generally a fabulous way to help increase your brand awareness in a community. For starters, simiply being invited means that someone already views you as an expert. The invitation itself is a tacit endorsement of your capabilities. Unless you tank, that endorsement will likely be received well by the attendees. Be sure to avoid the hard sell and provide ideas that are valuable to the audience. These types of events can be great opportunities to increase your email list or give out physical goodies to help build relationships.

Webinars

Webinars are a type of online speaking engagement. Some of the same rules apply: be wary of burdens of knowledge, provide value in what you're talking about, and avoid the hard sell. Be sure to test your technology the day before to help remove the chance of computer errors. The advantage of webinars over speaking engagements is that they can go anywhere and be easily recorded and shared after the event.

Live Events

Live events can offer you an opportunity to interact with your customers. Whether this be a lunch and learn, a trade show, or a conference that you put on, with a bit of investment, you can build great relationships. A good example of this is the Marketing AI conference put on by Paul Roetzer and PR 20/20. They established an arm of their company to begin talking about AI and then created a conference that would be used to help solidify their position as an expert. It also generates some sales of their courses and tickets. In person experiences can help motivate people to attend and give you an opportunity to further establish yourself as an expert. This can also dip into experiential marketing which we will talk about later in this book.

Social Media

Social Media is the ever present content monster always demanding more and more. Two things to think about when trying to keep up: 1. If you maximize your content, you will be looking at a variety of pieces for every one piece you make. 2. Document the daily life of your organization to help fill the gaps with pieces that are easy to make. Documentation is taking pictures of a meeting or showing what has recently arrived in a shipment. These quick pieces of content, when created with the customer in mind, can be great ways to help feed the social media beast.

Platforms

When picking social media platforms, start with where your customer's attention is. If your customers are all tweens, Linkedin might not be right. If you are dealing with all B2B sales with C Suite (executive level offices) folks, TikTok might not be right. We are not going to go into details here about which platforms are best for each demographic for one main reason: it changes all the time. New ones will emerge, old ones will lose favor, and customer bases will age and change their behavior. So the key concept here is to see where the attention is being spent by your audiences and invest there.

Content Strategy

How do you lay out your content to succeed? One of the keys is to understand your audience. What are they looking for? How can we entertain/educate/delight them?

Some emotions we can try to invoke from our

audience are: anger, awe, surprise, amusement, joy, sadness, laughter, inspiration, curiosity. Anger can be great for political campaigns and nonprofits, but maybe not a Heating and Air company.

The following list is long but it is not an exhaustive list of content types. These types of content can help give you some guidance on how to begin creating content:

Announcements, ask a question, expert opinion, get to know you, guides, holidays, how to, listicle, memes, polls, quizzes, testimonials, user generated content.

Mediums are the way we convey the information directed by the structure: Animation, audio, document, ebooks, graphics, interactive, live video, photography, stories, text video

Video Content

Blogs are not as useful as they used to be. As we consider how to put this content out, be sure to keep video at the top of your mind. It may be as simple as holding your phone and walking while talking. You may be in a situation to bring a production company or purchase a teleprompter to help ease this process. But in our culture today, video is key. So make sure it's part of your plan and that you are becoming comfortable being on camera. Side note: be sure to get captions for your video, as most videos on social are played without audio.

Making It Happen

Creating content is hard to do. For many organizations, it falls on the backburner when the business gets busy.

Make a Calendar- Look at a calendar setup to put content on a schedule that allows you to plan ahead for seasons when you may have more or less going on. Also, this can help you think through content that may have some seasonality to it.

Make someone responsible- Make sure someone knows it is their job to make this happen. This is an area where working with an outside firm can be helpful because they will help ensure things happen in a timely manner.

Set Reminders- Even something as simple as setting reminders on your phone can be helpful on a day to day basis.

While most of our builders are designed to convert incoming leads that come to you, sometimes you need help generating more traffic. This is where advertising comes into play.

Advertising is a paid opportunity to use networks other people have created to draw attention to your company. Newspapers and TV are classic examples of advertising. They create content people want to read, listen to, or watch and then charge advertisers a premium to get their message in with that same content. Facebook is no different. Facebook gives people a place to connect and express themselves, then capitalizes on the interaction to sell ads to advertisers. When we think about advertising, it is important to go back to our customer personas: Should we run ads for senior citizen targeted products on Instagram? Well, maybe not. But maybe we should run some ads on Facebook and in the local newspaper.

Digital Marketing

Digital Marketing is the standard in advertising these days. More and more of the budgets from major companies are being focused on digital marketing. Digital marketing is excelling for a few reasons. The main reason: It is where people's attention is. People are on their computers and phones more than ever; their attention is on their devices. Whether that be on YouTube, Facebook, the weather app, or their bank, so much of people's lives are seen through their devices. Additionally, digital marketing allows targeting in a way that legacy marketing (advertising options that existed before the internet) options never have. Being able to target someone by travel habits or the information they express other places online is a revelation to marketers.

Lastly, it is very affordable. Because of the scale,specificity of the marketing, and its ability to change quickly, the cost per purchase of advertising is a fraction of most legacy media. It is possible to create an ad campaign on Facebook for $10. Not so with legacy media.

Google Ads- One of the most powerful forms of advertising in the market is Google Search Ads. These ads appear when you do a Google search for something. At the top of the search list, an ad appears for a related product. While the ads are just text in this portion of the search, they can be very helpful. Why? Because the advertising is intent based. Unlike other forms of media, where it is largely demographically based, Google ads allow you to talk to someone as they are searching for your industry. It captures someone's attention in a moment when they might be prepared to make a purchase.

Social Media Ads

Social Media advertising is popular for a few reasons.

Big Brother Is Watching- Facebook, Instagram, Twitter, YouTube, etc. know a lot about you as an individual. They track everything you do on their platform - every video you watch and every image you linger on. All of this data gives them a robust profile of what you might want to purchase so they are able to serve you up ads on things you are interested in.

Social Proof- When ads are successful, you are able to acquire likes, comments, and shares that will travel with the ad on some platforms. These engagements show potential customers that other people like what they are seeing and that your company is legitimate. Additionally, some platforms can run ads that show a post with a comment above such as "Lauren also likes this page." Showing that other people interact with this brand can help bring validity. True story: this is one reason I started using the Best Self Journal years ago.

Social Proof is similar to Word of Mouth because it uses the credibility of your friends to help convince you to buy a product. Best Self Journal used Social Proof on Facebook ads that helped convince me to give them a try. I have now been using the journals for years!

Cost- The cost online is very scalable. The flexibility of the spending and the ability to turn it on and off yourself is attractive to small and large businesses alike.

Trackability- The old quip goes, "half my marketing works, I just don't know which half." One of the difficult aspects of marketing is showing your successes. With digital marketing in general, you are able to get very precise data about the reach and effectiveness of your advertising. The more digital your call to action is, the more you are able to track that ad to its conversion. This is one of the biggest reasons why people love digital marketing.

Retargeting- Remember going to a retail website and looking at an item like a shirt or a refrigerator and then seeing ads for it on Facebook later that night? That is called retargeting. Digital marketing allows for retargeting in a way that allows companies to make sure people see their ads multiple times which helps create conversions.

Native Feeling- While some forms of advertising are obviously not part of the content you are there to consume, other forms look like the content they surround. In the industry we call that Native Advertising. When you scroll through Facebook, you're not there to look at ads. But sometimes those ads look like something a friend might have shared. When ads look like content on the platform, that's called Native Advertising. Social media makes most of its advertising feel like native ads to make the messaging more effective.

Banner Ads and Geofencing

Banner ads are about as bold as it gets in digital marketing because they completely interrupt the user's experience. On your local news website, a banner might expand to cover the entire home page. On the app you use for free, it might suddenly stop what you're doing and take over the entire screen with a full screen spread or divide up the content you are there to see with bright colors or motion.

While they have some of the tracking and targeting capabilities of social media ads, they lack some subtlety that we feel hinders their effectiveness. There is no confusing them for native content and most of the time they are annoying. Because the ads are connected to the app that you are using, the permissions of the app you have such as GPS data is shared with the advertising. This allows for geofencing. Geofencing allows advertisers to draw lines around a map, sometimes as small as a singular property and only show advertising to people who have entered that geographic square. We do not generally endorse banner ads due to most people finding them annoying. However, the advantage they offer is that they are not tied to a social media account so they are able to reach people who are not on social media.

Influencers

Influencers are much like local news and radio stations. They use their content to build an audience of subscribers and viewers. They then use this audience to direct attention to advertisers. Advertisers enjoy this because they give access to very niche audiences of viewers. And when they advertise for brands, they give them a personal touch. It's like a radio DJ talking about a product (known as an ad-lib) as opposed to a prerecorded ad.

One of the odd things about the media is that if you consume someone's content enough, you get to feel like you know them or that you are friends. This, of course, is a completely one way relationship. The pyschological term for it is "parasocial interaction." But this relationship makes these ads more effective than ads disconnected from those same people.

The Others

There are more and more options for advertising online like Spotify, podcast sponsorships, Waze ads, sponsored content, etc. The key to each of these is to contemplate where your audience directs their attention.

Future Of Digital Marketing

At the time of writing this, the future of digital marketing is robust but cloudy. In the coming years, there will be an increasing focus on privacy online. The European Union led this direction with release of the GDPR (General Data Protection Regulation). This was the first major domino to fall in the wild west of digital advertising. GDPR made it hard for businesses in the EU to track and market to people. California has recently passed a GDPR inspired law called the CCPA. It is likely that the California law will inspire other states to follow.

What are likely to be as disruptive, if not more, are privacy moves by companies like Apple. As they said in a keynote recently, "the future is private." Many companies make money off our data, many that you and I have never heard of. Influential companies like Apple are in a unique position to directly affect this market by the technology they release. The next generations of Apple technology are likely to make their phone a data privacy machine rather than a data mining machine. And while most non-Apple people do not like to admit this, Apple generally sets the tone and standard for the future of the phone business.

What will the fallout be? It is hard to tell since marketing technology will not sit still as Apple and others make this move, they will counter attack. But likely some of the immense targeting options that currently exist will be hampered, especially those not tied to social networks, like banner ads. Also, privacy will become a premium product that will give companies like Apple a competitive advantage.

Legacy Marketing

Legacy Marketing includes things that have been around for more than 20 years ... before the Internet became widespread - things like newspaper ads, TV ads, billboards, and radio ads. These traditional media options for advertising remain strong while undergoing huge changes.

Advantages of Legacy- Demographics often decide for you whether to go with legacy or digital marketing. Traditional media outlets tend to perform better with older people. Traditional media can also address people who are online and people who aren't at the same time. If you are needing to target a very wide segment of the population, traditional marketing may help you achieve that.

Disadvantages of Legacy- Some of the weaknesses of these media have to deal with cost and tracking. Traditional media in most markets is still overpriced for the attention they deliver to advertisers. Digital is generally cheaper and faster to execute than traditional advertising. Lack of trackability with traditional advertising proves challenging. With digital, you can make your activity extremely trackable with URLs and pixels. Traditional methods lack these features. Also some of the legacy metrics they do use can be confusing or misleading.

Just because a newspaper has 30,000 subscriptions does not mean that 30,000 people saw your ad. But when you hear 30,000 you tend to think that many people saw your ad. In some smaller markets, TV and radio ratings are controlled by journaled markets. This means they rely on humans to write out their viewing behavior to see how things are performing, which is not as accurate as a Youtube view.

Future of Traditional

Two things will happen to legacy media in the future: 1. It is going to get cheaper. As the digital revolution rages on and the markets move away from focusing on traditional media, the cost per ad will need to decrease to be competitive. Over time, costs will decrease, making traditional advertising a better investment. The attention will match up with the cost. 2. For many of these media properties to survive they will get more digital in its capabilities like TV going digital and newspapers turning into apps. Then it will make more sense to invest in those platforms as well.

Sponsorships and Community Involvement

A great way to promote your company and invest

in your community is through community sponsorships. These range from sponsoring a nonprofit 5k, supporting your local Chamber of Commerce, or even helping the school system provide needed supplies for teachers.

Why should you spend your company dollars this way?

You are successful because your community purchases from you. Reinvesting with them is a sensible thing to do unless you are a robber baron (industrialists whose business practices were often considered ruthless or unethical). Reinvesting in your community allows the community to survive financially.

It allows you to activate an audience that cares about a topic. If you donate to a nonprofit that a subset of your community cares about, you are likely to build a relationship with that audience and increase word of mouth advertising.

It can be a way to help motivate your team. People care about more than just profitability; everyone has a social cause that they care about. If you can involve your team in the donations or at least sell them on the mission of the donation, it can help team morale, retain talent, make your organization an attractive place to work, and give them something to be proud of in their work. It is likely that you will get lots and lots of requests for sponsorship dollars. Consider what you care about to help winnow those requests down. If you are not passionate about music, maybe avoid giving to the orchestra, but if you are passionate about the visual arts, donate there. For example, Adelsberger Marketing works with CASA because my wife and I have been foster parents for years and are passionate about it.

A second way to be involved in the community is to allow your team members to serve on committees or boards. While there might not be a direct financial cost, sharing the brain and hands of your team with organizations that need them is important. Boards are a good way to give back and a nice way to network. Because everyone is there for the same reason, networking is natural in these situations. Networking can lead to new relationships, referrals, and talent acquisition.

Even though local media outlets have lost some of their marketing shine, it still pays to get free press for your business. Local media still touches a wide demographic but mostly older people consume it regularly. There is also a bit of clout that comes from newspaper coverage. Anyone can post on Facebook, not everyone can get in the newspaper. If your organization has something newsworthy, it's a good idea to put out a press release. You can find templates for press releases all over the internet. Keep in mind the goal with all marketing is to get someone's attention. If you write press releases about non newsworthy things or write them in a boring way, you are likely going to be ignored by the press.

Press releases are essentially news summaries for media outlets to review and consider. News organizations will republish press releases and some use it as a starting point for their content and will schedule an interview with your business. Any organization that might want to send press releases should start and update a list of potential media outlets to send press releases to. Since time is usually of the essence with the news, you will want this ready before you need it. In our small local market, we have lots of turnover in media staffing, so it's important to periodically update that list.

Relationships help get press releases covered. If you have provided good news events for outlets in the past, they will be more likely to work with you in the future. If you send pointless press releases regularly, it is more likely that you will get passed over or ignored in the future. Journalists work under demanding deadlines, so you may have to relax your expectations and work with them to get your press release published.

Also, look at other local organizations that might help you push out your press releases. Check with your local chamber of commerce. These organizations regularly share press releases from member businesses.

In the broad realm, a well placed story on a major news outlet or blog can turn someone's business fortunes quickly. If you earn exposure in a local news source, you usually get three coverages: The story in print/video, an article on their website, and a post on their social media page. Research the writers you want to contact and identify them by looking at their topics and see how you can contact them in a way that is meaningful to them. Consider what social media they use or things they care about. If there are multiple reporters to work with and one of them cares about dogs and our topic is about dogs, focus on that.

A lot of people want to talk to journalists, so make yourself stand out. Approach them via email/social/phone call with a concept for a story they can write about, or something that makes it unique. Be prepared for them, with time to talk, images they can use, or quotes they can pull. Make their life easier. Some sources print presses releases verbatim so be sure your press release is completely print ready - including all contact information, images, quotes, etc.

(This chapter is written with a pre/post COVID-19 world in mind. Clearly, in-person events have been affected by COVID-19 but it's unclear if they will be permanently affected.)

There is a difference between seeing and experiencing. Experiential marketing gives people a chance to go beyond seeing and get to know your product in a tangible way. This often happens when a friend shows you a product and you decide you want it, too. Recently my wife has considered getting an Apple Watch. She's seen me wear one and been able to try it out herself. Sam's Club, or "the Club" as I have heard it referred to, has been doing this for a long time. Walking through their store on a lucky day will give you the opportunity to try various different food products they are promoting. There have been multiple occasions when I have purchased the item I sampled.

When thinking about how to include experiential marketing into your plans, you can start somewhere small like a sample kiosk or delivering sample trays to businesses. Or you can go big like hosting an enormous conference such as (the conference formerly known as) Chick-fil-a Leadercast. Consider these questions when implementing these tactics:

What's your budget? Giving out samples at the store or setting up a pop-up tent at a local fair can be really affordable. Putting on a branded event for 100 people could be expensive. What you decide to do will be determined in part by your market value and your type of product. Maybe it involves sponsoring an event for a nonprofit, which would increase the cost but add social value. Will you need to bring in a partner organization like a food provider or a marketing company to help things be successful?

Does it align with your mission? Don't just do anything. Make sure it also aligns with your mission and company values. Our company invests almost exclusively in issues regarding foster care for children. So it might be a little outside our wheel well to host an event regarding animal welfare. But if your organization has a cause at its heart, you can combine the marketing of your organization with an event to benefit those things you care about.

Can you do it with excellence? If you are branching out into experiential marketing, can you do it well? A well executed event can add value to your brand. But if you invite 100 people for a test drive and the cars do not work right, you are potentially ruining the market for yourself. Do whatever it takes to ensure execution excellence. The more complicated the event, the more likely something will go wrong. Consider steps like rehearsals and dry runs of the event to help work out bugs. Hiring a professional event planner can be a worthy investment for companies.

Will it really promote your product? When planning an event, ensure that you don't forget to promote your product/service. I am sure you will not do that on purpose, but if your event overshadows what you are trying to do, or if it causes enough controversy to distract what you are trying to promote, you should rethink your approach.

Do people care? Consider this event from the perspective of someone who is an outsider to your business. If you are in a fun industry, this can be easy. But not everyone is. So do people care? You have to make it attractive to people who don't yet care. Try reaching across the aisle with a shared interest that can bridge the gap between your product and other people's interests. One of the best ways for a restaurant is to simply get a test bite into someone's mouth. If you produce food worth eating and give someone an opportunity to eat it, they easily become customers.

CHAPTER 7
OUR PILLARS OF MARKETING

I wanted to make note of what we have done to market Adelsberger Marketing. We have had success since opening in 2014 and as a marketing company, it is something we think about all the time.

One reason for our immediate success is that we came on the scene at the right time. Our affordable video options were something our market needed. Fulfill an unmet market need and your business will be set up for success. To realize that success, though, we had to market our marketing agency well. We have used a variety of builders and drivers to help grow the business. But we have really leaned on these three areas: community, expertise, and making stark raving fans.

Investing in our Community- Working with local organizations and nonprofits is great for serving your community by helping them do better work and promote themselves. It also exposes you to their base of support and board of directors. It's a great way to make connections. We support Madison County CASA because it is close to our hearts.

We work hard to stay involved with nonprofits in our area. Sometimes our involvement is as customers and sometimes as donors. In our earliest days, we did nonprofit projects for free. Today we often offer them discounts on services. I am also a graduate of the Leadership Jackson program and have remained active in it for years. Recently, we were able to strike a deal to become an annual sponsor of the program which gives us great visibility with many of the business leaders in our area.

Demonstrating our Expertise- We love the opportunity to educate people and help them grow their business or understanding of marketing and entrepreneurship. Very regularly we have had the opportunity to visit with and teach at theCO's CO.STARTERS program and the Economic Development day with Leadership Jackson. These give us opportunities to meet a lot of folks who become potential friends and customers. Additionally, we have had the opportunity to teach at different events and Chambers of Commerces across West Tennessee. Each one of these opportunities gives us the chance to meet new contacts and expand our business.

Making Stark Raving Fans- The most important thing we do for our marketing is building stark raving fans. Stark raving fans will tell others about your business which creates invaluable word of mouth. How do we do this? We strive to treat people right. Do what you say you are going to do, when you say you will, and at the price you commit to. Under promise and over deliver. If you make a mistake, make it right, even if it costs you money. Sometimes eating some cash to help correct a mistake is well worth the long run relationship that you have with clients. Always play for the long term. Short term gains can sometimes sacrifice long term success. If you nickel and dime customers, you will leave a bad taste in their mouths. We want to leave every customer with a great experience to encourage them to talk about us with their friends and be repeat customers. Think of each customer as a long term opportunity.

CHAPTER 9
CONCLUSION AND SUGGESTED READING

"Ideas are (expletive deleted), execution is the game." - Gary Vaynerchuk.

This book contains many thoughts on marketing. They are thoughts we use to grow our client's businesses. They work because we put them into action. We execute on these ideas. Many people have great ideas for content or marketing, but they fail to execute.

I hope you enjoyed this work, but more so hope that you will execute some concept from this book. Start with who you are and define it. Understand who your customers are and where they are in the process. Build the pieces you need to communicate with the world. Then, get someone's attention and motivate them to take your call to action.

If you found this valuable, consider leaving us a review on Facebook or Google. If you know you need to help with marketing, send me an email: kevin@adelsbergermarketing.com.

Thank you for your time and attention and don't forget how valuable both of those things are.

Kevin

References and Suggested Material:

I love reading so I prioritize it in my daily life. I find it's a great way to keep thinking about things that are helpful and also a great way to wind down from the day. Here are some of our top marketing books we recommend:

Juicing the Orange: Fallon- A great book talking about how a big deal advertising firm approaches creative.

Permission Marketing: Godin- In my opinion, this is the seminal book that shifted marketing from interruption to permission-based. Very formative. Also, just read everything Seth Godin has ever written.

Building a Storybrand: Miller- An excellent book on how to treat marketing writing to engage the reader and sell products.

Attention Merchants: Wu- A startling look at how

businesses have been selling our attention for decades, and increasingly so.

Ask Gary Vee: Vaynerchuk- Gary Vaynerchuk is the leader in social media marketing in my eyes. His books, including Crushing It, are excellent resources for anyone considering marketing in the modern era. He also has an enormous online presence and gives away a lot of information. He often sets the pace in online marketing.

The End of Advertising: Essex- A thoughtful look from inside the big ad system about how the system will change in the near future.

Breakthrough Advertising: Schwartz- A classic, but be warned, it's expensive online. It's insightful on the human condition. Originally published in 1966, some of the examples are dated but the core truths are applicable to all humankind.

Customers for Life: Sewell- My favorite book on customer service. In the book Carl Sewell talks about how he used customer service to build his dealerships. I can personally speak for these services and how we

were treated as out-of-towners in one of his dealerships.

About the Author

Kevin Adelsberger is the founder of Adelsberger Marketing where they make creative work that grows their clients' businesses in a culture that values their team and community of Jackson, Tennessee. After founding it in 2014, Kevin went on to be a co-founder of Our Jackson Home and host its podcast from 2015-2019.

In 2016, Kevin was recognized as an emerging leader by Leadership Jackson. In 2017, Adelsberger Marketing was named the Emerging Business of the Year by the Jackson Chamber. In 2019, Adelsberger Marketing sold partial ownership to Alexander, Thompson, and Arnold, CPAs. In 2020, Union University gave Kevin recognition for Distinquished Achievement in Arts and Media.

Kevin currently serves as the board president for Madison County CASA and is a board member for theCO in Jackson, Tennessee.

Kevin lives in Jackson with his wife and business partner, Renae, and their children. They are involved members of First Baptist Church, Jackson. They are also some of the few to cheer on the Minnesota Vikings from below the Mason-Dixon line.

Contact him at kevin@adelsbergermarketing.com